WALKABOUT

Changing Seasons

Editor: Ambreen Husain
Design: Volume One

Photographs: Heather Angel—6, 12, 17 inset, 31; Bruce Coleman Ltd.—(E. Crichton) 18, (P. Clement) 21, (H. Reinhard) 23; Eye Ubiquitous—(P. Prestidge) 4, (Skjold) 30; Chris Fairclough Colour Library 20, 24; Robert Harding—7; Frank Lane Picture Agency—(R. Wilmshurst) 11, (E. & D. Hosking) 17, (H. Clark) 29; George McCarthy—10; NHPA—(S. Dalton) 12 inset, (M. Grey) 16, (G. I. Bernard) 18 inset; Oxford Scientific Films—(J. Hallet) 8, (A. Ramage) 9, (B. Milne/Animals Animals) 28 inset; Superstock—13; Swift Picture Library—28, (M. King) 5; ZEFA—cover, 14, 15, 19, 22, 25, 26, 27.

Library of Congress Cataloging-in-Publication Data

Pluckrose, Henry Arthur.
Changing seasons / by Henry Pluckrose.
p. cm. — (Walkabout)
ISBN 0-516-08116-0
1. Nature—Juvenile literature. 2. Seasons—Juvenile literature. [1. Nature. 2. Seasons.] I. Title.
II. Series: Pluckrose, Henry Arthur. Walkabout.
QH81.P62 1994
508—dc20 93-44700
CIP
AC

1994 Childrens Press® Edition

Published simultaneously in Canada.
3 4 5 6 7 8 9 0 R 03 02 01 00 99 98 97 96

WALKABOUT
Changing Seasons

Henry Pluckrose

CHILDRENS PRESS ®
CHICAGO

The cold months of winter are over. Spring is here.

We know the signs of spring.
Trees bud and break into leaf.
The sun is higher in the sky.
It does not get dark so early.
The days grow warmer
and longer.

Gardens and parks are bright with spring flowers.

Soon, trees are in blossom.

Animals that sleep
through the winter
become active again.
The hedgehog leaves
its winter home
to hunt for food.

Frogs and toads lay their eggs in water.

Most birds build nests
to hold their eggs.
The parent birds sit on the
eggs to keep them warm
until they hatch.

When the eggs hatch, the baby birds must be fed.

Finding food in spring and early summer is much easier than in winter.

Slowly, spring
becomes summer.
The sun is high in the sky.
The days are longer and
there is more sunshine.
Often the weather is hot
and dry.

Colorful summer flowers come into bloom. Trees are full of leaves . . .

and fruit grows fat and juicy.

Young animals and birds leave their nests. They learn how to find food, how to climb, swim, and fly.

Wheat and barley ripen in the fields. Summer fruits are ready to be picked.

As summer ends, farmers harvest their crops.

Slowly, summer becomes fall.
The days grow shorter and nights grow longer.
The sun is lower in the sky.
Cooler weather comes and many birds fly away to spend the winter in warmer places.

Squirrels, mice, and voles are busy gathering food. They store it away to eat in the winter.

Farmers prepare the fields for the next year's crop.

Apples and pears are picked and stored . . . if they do not get eaten first!

The leaves of many trees start to turn red, orange, yellow, and brown.

Birds and small animals feast on berries. Juicy blackberries grow on thorny bushes.

Frost sparkles on leaves
and branches.
The sun gives
little warmth.
Many trees are bare.
It is winter.

Few plants grow in winter.
Seeds lie in the cold
ground, waiting for the
warmth of spring.
But the cold does not stop
all flowers from growing . . .
snowdrops push their way up—
even through snow.

It is difficult for animals and birds to find enough food in winter.

Some animals go to sleep. The deer mouse finds a warm sheltered place to spend the winter.

A heavy fall of snow makes everything look different. If we wear warm clothes, snow and ice can be fun!

Slowly, the seasons change.
Winter is turning
into spring.
Plants begin to push up
through the soil.
Animals begin to stir.
Once more it is spring.

Index

animals, 8, 16, 25, 28, 29, 31
apples, 23
barley, 18
berries, 25
birds, 10, 11, 16, 20, 25, 28
blackberries, 25
blossoms, 7, 15
branches, 26
bushes, 25
crops, 19, 22
days, 5, 13, 20
deer mouse, 29
eggs, 9, 10, 11
fall, 20
farmers, 19, 22
fields, 18, 22
flowers, 6, 14, 27
food, 8, 12, 16, 21, 28
frogs, 9
frost, 26
fruits, 15, 18
gardens, 6
hedgehog, 8
leaves, 5, 14, 24, 26
mice, 21
nests, 10, 16
nights, 20
parks, 6
pears, 23
plants, 27, 31
seeds, 27
sky, 5, 13, 20
snow, 27, 30
snowdrops, 27
soil, 31
spring, 4, 5, 12, 13, 27, 31
squirrels, 21
summer, 12, 13, 14, 18, 19, 20
sun, 5, 13, 20, 26
sunshine, 13
toads, 9
trees, 5, 7, 14, 24, 26
voles, 21
water, 9
weather, 13, 20
wheat, 18
winter, 4, 8, 12, 20, 21, 26-29, 31

About this book

Young children acquire information in a casual, almost random fashion. Indeed, they learn just by being alive! The books in this series complement the way young children learn. Through photographs and a simple text the readers are encouraged to comment on the world around them.

To a young child, the world is new and almost everything in it is interesting. But interest alone is not enough. If a child is to grow intellectually this interest has to be directed and extended. This book uses a well-tried and successful method of achieving this goal. By focusing on a particular topic, it invites the reader first to look and then to question. The words and photographs provide a starting point for discussion.

Children enjoy information books just as much as stories and poetry. For those who are not yet able to read print, this book provides pictures that encourage talk and visual discrimination—a vital part of the learning process.

Henry Pluckrose

CHILDRENS PRESS

U.S. $4.95
Can. $6.95